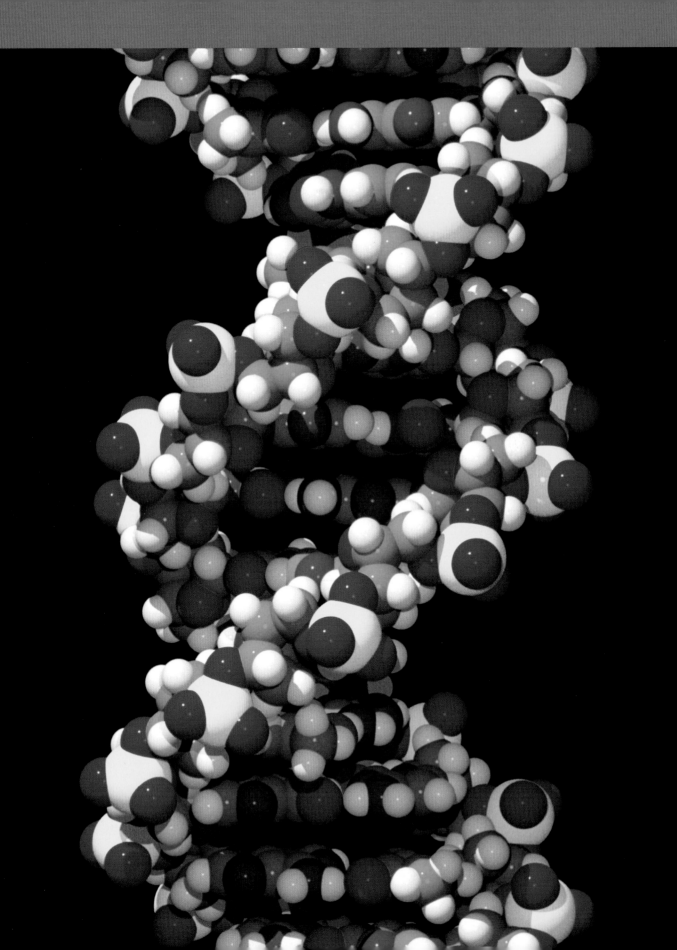

NATIONAL GEOGRAPHIC Washington D.C.

Double Helix

The Quest to Uncover the Structure of DNA

Glen Phelan

The science of heredity started with a curious gardener in a pea patch.

CONTENTS

9 INTRODUCTION

13 CHAPTER 1
THE SCIENCE GARDEN

19 CHAPTER 2
PICKING UP THE TRAIL

25 CHAPTER 3
THE RACE FOR DNA

35 CHAPTER 4
WHO WILL WIN?

45 CHAPTER 5
PRIZES, GLORY, AND MORE WORK

55 GLOSSARY

56 RESOURCES

58 INDEX

Crick (left) and Watson at Cambridge.

INTRODUCTION

On February 28, 1953, Francis Crick walked into a pub in Cambridge, England, and made a startling announcement. He and his colleague, James Watson, had just discovered "the secret of life." He wasn't kidding! Earlier that day, Watson and Crick had figured out the structure of a mysterious substance called DNA.

Bowling was a popular family entertainment in the 1950s.

Life in the 1950s

The 1950s were a time of booms—baby booms, buying booms, building booms, and technology booms. What brought all of this about? The hard times of the Great Depression and World War II were over. More people were going to college and getting good jobs. They were moving into new homes in the suburbs and raising large families. People wanted to have fun—and there were plenty of products to please them. Buyers gobbled up small transistor radios, TVs, and big, new cars.

1822

Gregor Mendel is born.

Many families took road trips in their new cars.

But life in the 1950s was more than just gadgets and gizmos. Breakthroughs were being made in the life sciences, too. Scientists were developing new medicines to fight diseases such as influenza (the flu) and polio. And many physicists and chemists were getting involed in the life sciences. In particular, they were interested in genetics, a branch of biology that studies inherited traits and variation of organisms. It was at that time that Watson and Crick discovered the structure of DNA. It was a huge breakthrough, because until scientists understood the structure of DNA, they weren't able to tell how genetic information was passed on.

Many of these scientists didn't know much about genetics at first. But they did know of Gregor Mendel, an Austrian monk who became known as "The Father of Genetics," all because of his interest in pea plants.

science BOOSTER

What Is DNA?

DNA is the substance in your cells that carries information about all of your inherited characteristics, or traits. Half of your DNA comes from your mother. The other half comes from your father. In fact, every living thing— from a pig to a potato plant— has its own DNA that passes from parent to offspring.

Today scientists study DNA to find cures for diseases, develop new sources of food, even to identify criminals.

In the garden of this monastery in Brno, in what is now the Czech Republic, Mendel experimented on pea plants.

THE SCIENCE GARDEN

In 1856, Gregor Mendel started an experiment unlike any conducted before. It took several years, and Mendel was unsure if he would be able to complete it. He had many questions, but he hoped his experiment of planting seeds and tending to the resulting pea plants would provide some of the answers. He had no idea that his work in the garden would lead to a whole new field of study.

Escape routes used by slaves seeking freedom became known as the Underground Railroad.

> Mendel kept careful records. And before long, he began to notice some patterns.

Growing Up to Teach

Gregor Mendel knew a lot about growing things. As a boy, he helped his father take care of the gardens that fed the family. He loved making things grow. When Mendel was old enough, he joined the monastery in his town to become a monk. The monks worked as teachers. Mendel himself had not gone to school regularly as a boy, so as a young adult, he was not prepared to take the exams to become a teacher. In fact, he failed the tests two times.

But the abbot, or leader of the monastery, knew that Mendel was bright. So the abbot sent him to college to learn math and science, two subjects that greatly interested Mendel. Soon he became a teacher, but what he loved most was taking care of the gardens in the monastery. He was curious about what he saw growing there. For example, he wondered why some pea plants had green seeds and some had yellow seeds. Some pea plants had flowers only at the top, and some had flowers only along the sides. These were all the same kinds of plants, yet they looked so different from each other and had such different traits. Mendel simply had to find out why.

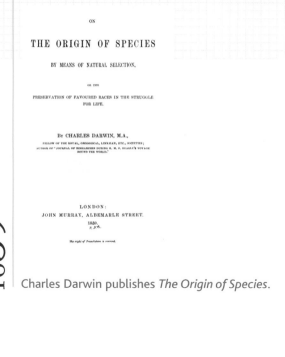

ON

THE ORIGIN OF SPECIES

BY MEANS OF NATURAL SELECTION,

OR THE

PRESERVATION OF FAVOURED RACES IN THE STRUGGLE
FOR LIFE.

By CHARLES DARWIN, M.A.,
FELLOW OF THE ROYAL, GEOLOGICAL, LINNÆAN, ETC., SOCIETIES;
AUTHOR OF 'JOURNAL OF RESEARCHES DURING H. M. S. BEAGLE'S VOYAGE
ROUND THE WORLD.'

LONDON:
JOHN MURRAY, ALBEMARLE STREET.
1859.

The right of Translation is reserved.

1859

Charles Darwin publishes *The Origin of Species*.

Mendel at work in his garden

Mendel set aside a plot of land in the monastery gardens. For the next seven years, he grew pea plants and observed them carefully. He cross-bred some plants. (That's the process of taking the pollen from one plant and using it to fertilize another plant.) Mendel kept careful records. Before long, he began to recognize some patterns.

In one experiment, Mendel cross-bred a tall pea plant with a short pea plant. The resulting seeds all grew into tall pea plants. What had happened to the trait of shortness? Mendel thought it must be hidden there in the plants. When he planted the seeds from these tall plants, he got another surprise. About three-fourths of the plants were tall, and one-fourth were short. The shortness trait had reappeared!

Mendel's work
was forgotten for
about 35 years.

1884

Gregor Mendel dies.

Fun Fact

Mendel also experimented with several other traits. Each time he found the same pattern. He thought that each trait was controlled by tiny "factors." (Today, we call Mendel's factors *genes*.) One factor for a trait comes from the male parent, and the other factor comes from the female parent. Mendel also thought that some factors were more powerful than others. He called these more powerful factors *dominant* and the less powerful ones *recessive*. A recessive factor produced its trait only if it paired up with another recessive factor. Mendel's experiments showed that tallness in pea plants is dominant, and shortness is recessive.

Forgotten Ideas

Gregor Mendel's work was unique. No one else had ever taken the time and the care to study living things in this way.

Other scientists at the time did not appreciate Mendel's work. When he read a report about his results at a scientific meeting, there was silence. No questions. No comments. No congratulations. He was practically ignored. His report was published, but no one paid much attention. His ideas seemed too simple. Also, since he lived in a monastery, Mendel was isolated, off in a world of his own. There was no exchange of ideas as there was at universities, where most scientific work was done.

So, Mendel's work was forgotten for about 35 years. But other scientists who had never heard of Mendel started similar experiments of their own. In 1900, several scientists came to the same conclusions Mendel had. When they learned about the work Mendel had done in the same area, they gave him credit for their findings. They said that their experiments confirmed what he had done.

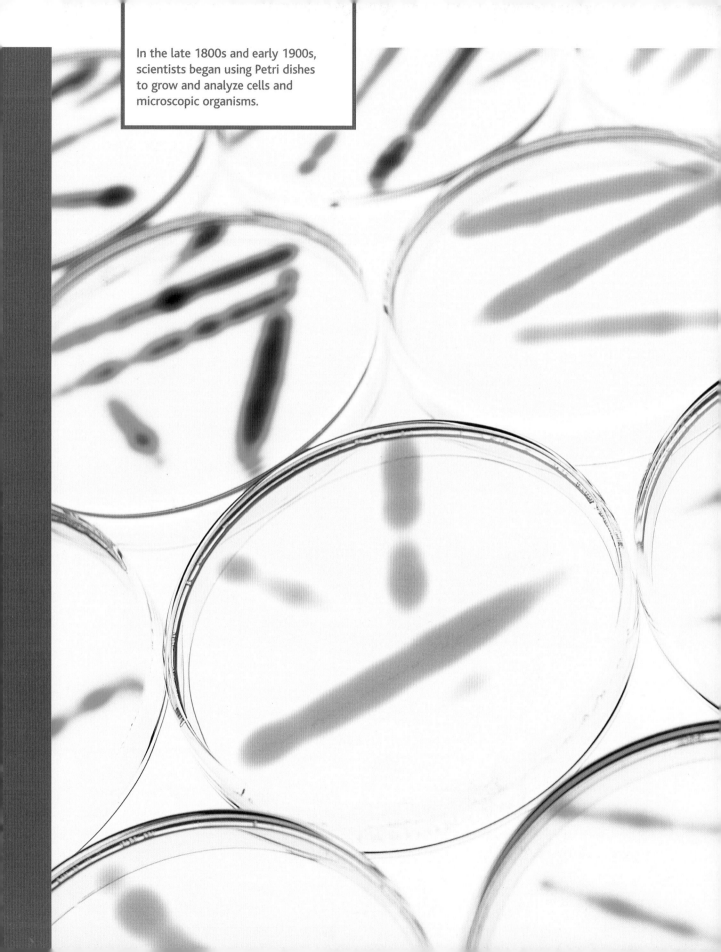

In the late 1800s and early 1900s, scientists began using Petri dishes to grow and analyze cells and microscopic organisms.

PICKING UP THE TRAIL

If you had lived in the early 1900s, you would have seen amazing things—such as the first airplanes and cars! Progress was being made in the life sciences, too. Scientists were finding the causes of deadly diseases, such as scarlet fever and the measles. The medicines to prevent these diseases were hailed as miracles.

1885
Scientists locate chromosomes in cells.

1901
Linus Pauling is born.

1900
Gregor Mendel's work is confirmed.

While some scientists were probing the mysteries of disease, others were looking into the mysteries of DNA and heredity. By the early 1900s, scientists knew some things about DNA. They knew that it was a large molecule of several kinds of bonded atoms. They also knew what it was made of. By the late 1900s, they knew that it was located in the chromosomes—long strands in the nucleus of each cell. That was an important piece of information, because scientists knew that chromosomes were involved with heredity. Could DNA be the special material that genes were made of? Some scientists thought so, but others disagreed.

What Are Genes Made Of?

In 1928, British scientist Frederick Griffith (right) came one step closer to finding out that genes are made of DNA, but he did so by accident. Griffith was trying to find out how bacteria cause pneumonia. Instead, he found that one kind of bacterium can pass its genetic material to another kind of bacterium. What was this genetic material?

It wasn't until 1944 that a group of scientists answered that question. They ran experiments that proved that DNA is that genetic material.

At last, scientists had discovered that genes are made of DNA. But a question remained: How does DNA carry information from parent to offspring? Scientists were sure the answer lay in the structure of DNA. They wanted to figure out what DNA looks like—how it's put together—so they could figure out how it works. That would be the secret of life!

Pneumonia bacteria seen under a microscope

1903

The Wright Brothers launch the first successful airplane flight at Kitty Hawk, North Carolina.

1909

Wilhelm Johannsen first uses the word "gene" in relation to heredity.

1916

Francis Crick is born.

Maurice Wilkins is born

The Contestants Gather

A competitive tennis player, a brilliant bird-watcher, an inspired researcher, and an x-ray expert. They were different ages and had different backgrounds. But their work came together at the same point in time, and whether they liked it or not, they were on the same mission!

People from many different fields of science soon wanted to work on DNA. During World War II, a lot of physicists and chemists helped the war effort by working on military equipment and on weapons. Some scientists helped design the first nuclear bombs. After the war, a number of scientists decided that they wanted to study life instead of weapons. They welcomed the DNA challenge.

So the 1950s began with a flurry of excitement. Science was on the brink of figuring out how DNA works—and breaking the genetic code. Each breakthrough in research brought the answer a bit closer, and most scientists wanted to be part of the effort. The race was on!

science BOOSTER

What Is a Gene?
Mendel called them "factors," but a gene carries all the information for how a living thing grows. Genes are passed from parents to offspring. That means that your parents' genes determine if you'll be short or tall, what color eyes you'll have, and even if your hair will be straight or curly.

James Watson

BORN April 26, 1928,
Chicago, Illinois

As a young boy in Chicago, one of James Watson's hobbies was bird-watching. He loved to spend time reading books about birds and learning as much as he could about them. James liked to read books on just about any subject.

James was so smart that he enrolled in the University of Chicago when he was just 15 years old. He then earned a Ph.D. in zoology from Indiana University in 1950, when he was 22 years old. Then he went to England, where he met Francis Crick and the rest is history.

After the discovery of the structure of DNA, Watson taught in the United States for many years. In 1988, he began directing the Human Genome Project. The project has identified 20,000–25,000 genes in the human DNA and made them accessible for further study. Today, Watson is President of the Cold Spring Harbor Laboratory, a research and educational institution in New York.

Francis Crick

BORN June 8, 1916,
Northhampton, England

DIED July 28, 2004,
San Diego, California

Francis Crick loved science from the time he was a boy. He also loved sports, including soccer, rugby, tennis, and cricket. He was extremely inquisitive about most things, and his parents had trouble keeping up with all the questions Francis would ask. The encyclopedia they gave him as a gift only fueled Crick's curiosity. He spent a lot of free time conducting experiments, including one where he tried to make artificial silk.

Crick studied physics in school. During World War II, he worked on developing explosive mines. After the war, he began to study biology. His famous partnership with James Watson actually started because Crick had a reputation for being nosy and talkative, and Watson was one of the few people who would share a lab bench with him!

Crick earned his Ph.D. in 1954, and in 1962 he shared the Nobel Prize for his work on DNA with James Watson. Later, in the 1970s, he began to focus his research on the brain.

Watson

Crick

Watson and Crick worked at Cambridge University, in England.

THE RACE FOR DNA

In England in the early 1950s, two pairs of scientists were working on the DNA mystery. James Watson and Francis Crick made up one pair. They worked in Cambridge, England, about 50 miles north of London. Watson and Crick got along very well. They shared information and bounced ideas off each other. They made a good team. Maurice Wilkins and Rosalind Franklin made up the other pair.

Crick on vacation with his wife, Odile, and daughter, Gabrielle.

Crazy About Science

Young Francis Crick couldn't accept an explanation if it didn't make sense to him. He might say, "But that can't be right," and then give what he thought was the right explanation. From playing with chemistry sets to collecting wildflowers, Francis liked all kinds of science and had decided at an early age that he wanted to become a scientist. But he was worried that by the time he grew up, everything would be discovered. "Don't worry," his mother said. "There will be plenty left for you to find out."

1920 Rosalind Franklin is born.

1928 James Watson is born.

When he grew up, he worked in physics before turning to biology. While at Cambridge University, he became interested in the mysteries of DNA.

Finding a New Challenge

James Watson got his Ph.D. at the age of 22 by doing a study on viruses. Then one day in Italy, he heard Maurice Wilkins give a lecture about DNA. He was hooked. Watson decided then and there that he would try to solve the mystery of DNA. In 1951, James Watson teamed up with Francis Crick at Cambridge. Watson was only 23 years old. Crick was 35.

science BOOSTER

Fun Fact
One of the other scientists trying to discover the structure of DNA was a famous chemist named Linus Pauling. Much of what Watson and Crick knew about chemistry came from textbooks that Pauling had written.

Maurice Wilkins

BORN December 15, 1916, Pongaroa, New Zealand

DIED October 5, 2004, London, England

When Maurice Wilkins was six, his father moved the family from New Zealand to Birmingham, England. Despite the early transition, Maurice considered himself to be a true New Zealander. And he believed that growing up in the country, where there were so many new and different things to discover, helped fuel his curiosity for science.

Wilkins studied physics at Cambridge and earned a Ph.D. in 1940. During World War II, he worked on bombs. After the war, he lectured at St. Andrew's University in Scotland and then moved to King's College in London. His work with x-ray pictures helped Watson and Crick discover the structure of DNA. In 1962, he shared the Nobel Prize with Watson and Crick for this work.

1939–1945

World War II

An X-ray Expert

Maurice Wilkins had worked on the atomic bomb during World War II. Like Crick, he was a physicist who switched to biology after the war. In his research, Wilkins was trying to figure out the structure of DNA by shooting x-rays through it. The x-rays made an image of the DNA on film. It was enough to offer clues, but it was more of a shadowy outline than a complete picture. Wilkins showed these ghostly images at his lecture in Italy—the one that got James Watson interested in DNA.

At that time doctors were using x-rays to take pictures of people's bones. Scientists were using x-rays to study minerals and other solids. Wilkins was using a technique called x-ray diffraction to study DNA, but the technique needed a lot of work. So Wilkins's boss hired one of the leading experts on this technique—Rosalind Franklin.

When Watson joined Crick at Cambridge in 1951, Wilkins and Franklin were already hard at work on DNA.

Rosalind Franklin

BORN July 25, 1920, London, England

DIED April 16, 1958, London, England

Rosalind Franklin decided to become a scientist when she was 15 years old. But her father disapproved of higher education for women and wanted her to become a social worker. Rosalind and her mother argued that she should be allowed continue her education, and her father finally gave in.

Rosalind received a Ph.D. in chemistry in 1945. In 1947 she went to Paris, where she learned x-ray diffraction techniques. She returned to England in 1951 and began work at King's College in London with Maurice Wilkins.

Later in her life, Rosalind headed a research group at Birkbeck College in London. Her research helped to lay the foundation in the field of structural virology.

1948

The first Polaroid cameras are sold.

1945

Scientists show genes are made of DNA.

More Than a Misunderstanding

Franklin started working on DNA at King's College in 1951. She had been hired to work with Maurice Wilkins. But Wilkins didn't see it that way. He thought of her as an assistant, someone who was working *for* him, not *with* him. It was hard to be a woman scientist in those days. For example, only men were allowed in some of the university dining rooms. After work, many of the male scientists went to men-only pubs. Scientists often shared ideas in these informal settings. They also built friendships and trust—important parts of teamwork. All of these traditions made it hard for Franklin to work with her fellow scientists in the same way.

Wilkins didn't make it any easier. The two did not get along. They disagreed on many issues—such as what kind of DNA to use in their experiments. Although Franklin and Wilkins both did excellent work, they did much of it separately.

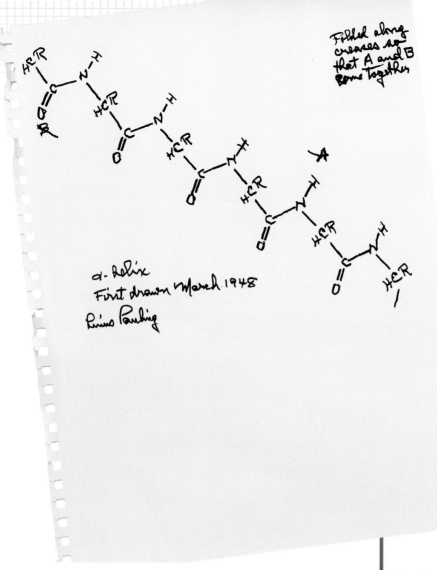

α-helix
First drawn March 1948
Linus Pauling

Filled along creases so that A and B come together

Linus Pauling made this drawing during his study of protein structures. His models and drawings inspired Watson and Crick to think about the structure of DNA.

Building Models

While Wilkins and Franklin were making x-ray pictures, Watson and Crick were building three-dimensional models. They were following the example of Linus Pauling. Pauling was a famous American chemist. Among other things, he had found the cause of a disease called sickle-cell anemia. And he had used models to find out how molecules were put together. Now Pauling was working on models of DNA. Watson and Crick agreed with Pauling that fiddling around with models was the best way to figure out DNA's structure.

Crick (left) and Watson made a great team.

Scientists already had some pretty good ideas about the DNA molecule. They knew there were six parts that had to somehow fit together. They knew the shapes of the parts, and that some of the parts formed long strands. They speculated on how far apart the atoms were and how they joined. Finally, they thought that the structure had to show how the DNA molecule could copy itself many times. After all, that was how the DNA passed from parent to offspring.

1950

The Korean War begins.

science BIOGRAPHY

Linus Pauling

BORN **February 28, 1901, Portland, Oregon**

DIED **August 19, 1994, Big Sur, California**

As a child, Linus Pauling loved collecting bugs and rock and mineral samples. In high school, a friend introduced him to chemistry. His teachers noticed his fascination and let him conduct experiments.

After receiving a Ph.D. in chemistry in 1925, he taught and researched for nearly 40 years at the California Institute of Technology. His work with molecules earned him great recognition. In 1954, he won the Nobel Prize in Chemistry for his work on chemical bonds.

In addition to science, Linus was interested in social issues. He traveled the world campaigning against nuclear weapons, and in 1962, he won the Nobel Peace Prize.

Clues and Near Misses

Watson and Crick were working hard on their models. They had the university metal shop make a bunch of flat pieces of tin in certain shapes. They gathered wire, metal rods, and clamps. Then they started playing with the pieces. They thought that DNA was shaped like some sort of helix, or spiral. But their first models were way off the mark. Often the angles were wrong. Sometimes the pieces didn't match up. Sometimes the model just didn't make sense.

But Watson and Crick were learning from their mistakes. They knew that there were many ways to solve a problem. If one way wasn't working, they tried another. They could also disagree in a friendly way. Watson might suggest an idea. Then Crick might say, "but that can't be right," just as he might have when he was a boy. But that was OK. They both felt like kids at times. To them, solving the DNA mystery was one big adventure. Then suddenly, it looked like the adventure was over.

In this molecular model of DNA, individual atoms are depicted as spheres. White represents hydrogen; black represents carbon; blue represents nitrogen; red represents oxygen; and yellow represents phosphorus.

WHO WILL WIN?

4

"Almost there!" That's what Watson and Crick thought in December 1951. There were a few details to add, but they had built a model they thought worked well. They invited Wilkins and Franklin to Cambridge to get their opinions. Watson and Crick were expecting them to be impressed. Instead, the day turned into a disaster.

1952

Elizabeth Alexandra Mary Windsor is crowned Queen Elizabeth II of Great Britain.

1951

J.D. Salinger's *The Catcher in the Rye* is published.

A Flawed Model

As Wilkins and Franklin reviewed the model, it became clear that it was wrong. Watson had used information from one of Franklin's lectures to build the model. He had a bad habit of depending on his memory instead of taking good notes. He had incorrectly remembered some information from the lecture. And that was the one thing that made the model wrong. It was embarrassing. Watson and Crick's boss was so mad that he took them off the project. There were other things for them to do. Besides, their boss said, the DNA project belonged to Wilkins and Franklin. So, for more than a year, Watson and Crick pretty much stayed away from their models. Meanwhile, Linus Pauling was going full speed ahead. It seemed certain that Pauling would win the race to discover the structure of DNA.

Watson and Crick explain their model of DNA.

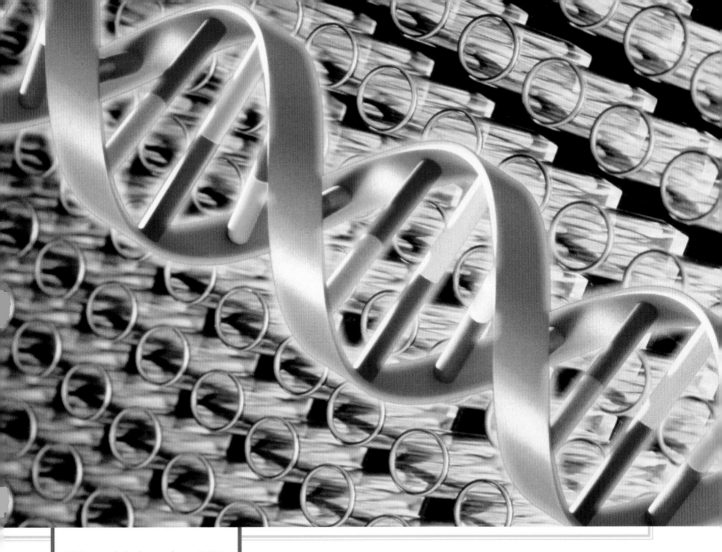

This model shows how DNA bases bond. DNA strands are connected by four bases. These bases are complex molecules called adenine, thiamine, guanine, and cytosine. Each base pairs up with its complementary base by hydrogen bonding. Adenine pairs up with thiamine, and guanine pairs up with cytosine.

Pauling in the Lead

In late 1952, Linus Pauling built his own model of DNA. Watson and Crick nervously waited to see what he would come up with. When they read the report, they let out a sigh of relief. They could tell right away that his model was wrong. But they knew Pauling was hot on the trail.

Not that they wished him any bad luck. But the search for DNA's structure had become a huge competition. Watson and Crick tried to convince Wilkins and Franklin to work with models. They even offered to give them some of their model-building equipment. But Wilkins and Franklin preferred to study DNA with their x-ray photos.

This x-ray, taken by Rosalind Franklin, was enough for Watson to realize that DNA is shaped in a double helix.

Those photos were getting better and better, providing more clues about DNA. But Wilkins and Franklin weren't sharing their information just yet. Franklin was a very careful scientist. She wanted to study the photos more before showing them to anyone else. She even kept some of her work from Wilkins. But what Franklin didn't know was that in the spring of 1953, Wilkins showed one of her best x-ray photos to James Watson.

A Picture Is Worth a Thousand Words

When Watson saw the photograph, he could hardly believe it. "The instant I saw the picture, my mouth fell open, and my pulse began to race," Watson wrote. He hurried back to his boss and got permission to study DNA again. Watson and Crick were back in the model-building business.

Why was Watson so excited about Franklin's photo? It showed that the DNA molecule was made of not one, but

1953

Watson and Crick propose
double helix model of DNA

1954

The Tournament of Roses Parade
is the first show to be broadcast
in color on television.

1955

Rosa Parks refuses to give
up her seat on a bus, sparking
a year-long bus boycott in
Montgomery, Alabama.

two spiraling chains —a double helix. And it showed that the
other parts of the molecule were in between these chains.

The photo was the break that Watson and Crick needed.
Just a few weeks later, they finished building their model
of DNA. It was a wobbly, odd-looking thing. But to
Watson and Crick, it was beautiful.

Across the Finish Line

Watson and Crick reported their findings in the April 25,
1953, issue of the British science journal *Nature*. Articles by
Wilkins and Franklin about their x-ray diffraction studies
appeared in the same issue. Together, the articles provided
the crucial evidence that supported the model. The model fit
everything that was then known about DNA: even though
it's large, it's a simple molecule.

science BOOSTER

Fun Fact

When Watson and Crick sent
in their article to *Nature*,
they had to decide whose
name would appear first.
What do you think would be
a fair way to do it?

That's right, they flipped a
coin. If the toss had gone the
other way, you'd instead be
reading "Crick and Watson"
throughout the book.

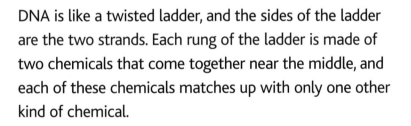

A computer model shows how DNA begins to copy itself in a cell by breaking apart like a zipper.

DNA is like a twisted ladder, and the sides of the ladder are the two strands. Each rung of the ladder is made of two chemicals that come together near the middle, and each of these chemicals matches up with only one other kind of chemical.

The model also showed how DNA copies itself. Basically, the molecule "unzips." The twisted ladder becomes two half-ladders. Each half of the ladder is a pattern for new chemicals that attach to it. When all the chemicals move into place, there are two twisted ladders, or spirals of DNA. Each spiral is exactly the same as the original.

This model shows the backbones of complementry strands of DNA as red and blue rods. The backbones are made of sugar. They are connected together by nitrogenous bases, depicted as gold bars.

This machine is a laboratory robot. It's performing the task of replica-plating, where some cells are taken from wells in one plate and moved to wells in an identical plate. This results in two well-plates containing the same cells. Replica-plating allows scientists to perform different types of tests on identical cells.

PRIZES, GLORY, AND MORE WORK

When the mystery of DNA's structure was finally solved, everyone was thrilled—Watson, Crick, Wilkins, Franklin, and Pauling. They all knew the discovery would change the life sciences forever.

1958

Rosalind Franklin dies.

1962

Linus Pauling wins the Nobel Peace Prize (above). Watson, Crick, and Wilkins win the Nobel Prize for Medicine.

1963

The vaccine for measles becomes available.

Fame

The discovery of "the secret of life" brought fame, glory, and a Nobel Prize. In 1962, James Watson, Francis Crick, and Maurice Wilkins shared the Nobel Prize for medicine for discovering the structure of DNA. One person was missing from this list—Rosalind Franklin. Sadly, Franklin's life was cut short. She died of cancer in 1958, when she was only 37 years old. If she had lived, she, too, would have received the Nobel Prize. Linus Pauling also received the Nobel Prize in 1962. But it was the Nobel Peace Prize, which he won for his efforts to ban the testing of nuclear weapons. He organized a petition that included the signatures of more than 11,000 scientists from 49 countries. His efforts led to a test ban treaty in 1963.

> The discovery of "the secret of life" brought fame, glory, and a Nobel Prize.

Maurice Wilkins (left), Francis Crick (3rd from left), and James James Watson (2nd from right) receive their 1962 Nobel Prizes.

Following Dreams

You might think that Watson and Crick would have kept working together. After all, they were such a good team. But even with their big discovery, they both had other interests they wanted to pursue.

Watson went to the California Institute of Technology for a few years. There he used x-rays to study other molecules. He worked with Crick again briefly before going to teach at Harvard University.

A scientist works to decode DNA sequences.

Linus Pauling continued to teach after the race to find the structure of DNA was over.

1972

Richard M. Nixon is re-elected U.S. President.

Moving On

Crick continued to study DNA and genetics at Cambridge until the 1970s. Then he moved to southern California to work at the Salk Institute, where he did research on the brain. He was especially interested in how the brain interacts with our eyes to give us sight. Just as he had helped to discover the structure of DNA, Crick wanted to make similar contributions to brain research. He knew exciting discoveries would be made.

1988 British citizen Colin Pitchfork becomes the first person convicted of a crime using DNA fingerprinting evidence.

1988 The Human Genome Project is launched.

Our knowledge of DNA has led to our ability to change, or engineer, DNA.

Maurice Wilkins stayed at King's College for many years. He continued to use x-rays to study nerve cells. Franklin, however, never felt comfortable at the college. She didn't think her colleagues took her seriously as a scientist. Soon after the DNA discovery in 1953, Franklin went to another college in London, where she studied the structures of viruses. She and Francis Crick often went to each other for advice and to share their discoveries. Franklin was finally being taken seriously as a scientist. People recognized not only her superb work but also her courage. She never complained about her illness. Rosalind Franklin continued to do research until a few weeks before her death in 1958.

R1440

R3089

C451

R1357

Genetic maps graph the arrangement of genes on a chromosome.

DNA Today

The discovery that Watson and Crick made has been called the most important event in biology in the last one hundred years. It opened up the field of modern genetics and will surely continue to provide fascinating new research for the next one hundred years as well.

Our knowledge of DNA has led to our ability to change, or engineer, DNA. This science of genetic engineering has opened up many possibilities that have yet to be fully explored. Someday, we may be able to find the causes — and the cures—for inherited diseases. We'll learn more about other diseases, such as cancer. We will make new medicines. The list goes on and on.

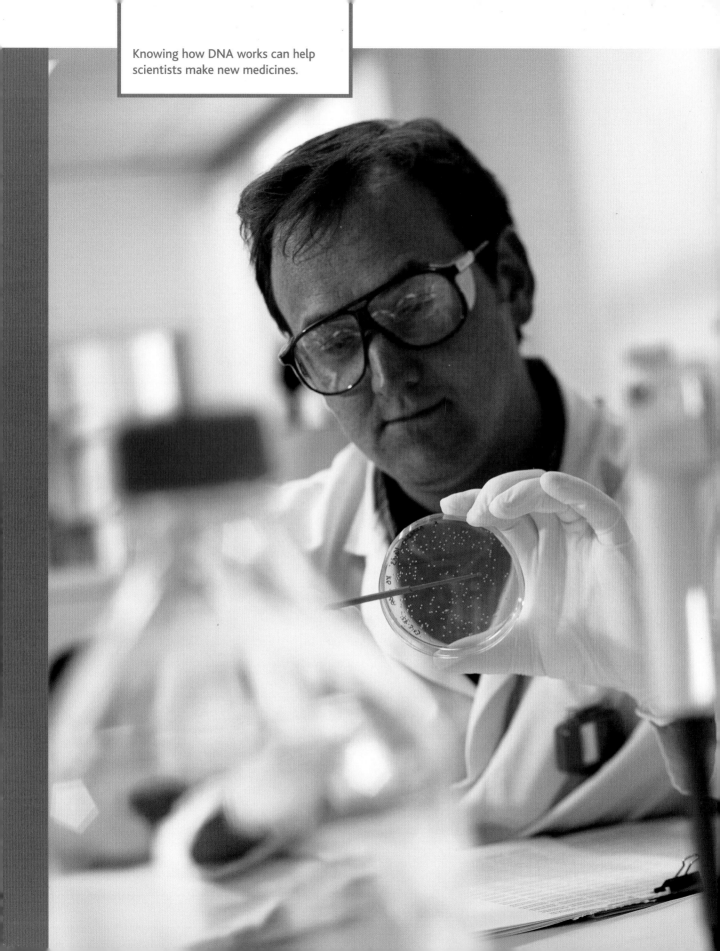

Knowing how DNA works can help scientists make new medicines.

1994

Linus Pauling dies.

2004

Francis Crick dies.

Maurice Wilkins dies.

The Joy of Discovery

In some respects, the way that the structure of DNA was discovered is just as important as the discovery itself. The people who made discoveries about DNA and heredity did not learn everything all at once. They kept asking questions and seeking answers. For example, Gregor Mendel was not afraid to tackle a long, careful experiment. Rosalind Franklin wanted to be taken seriously as a scientist, and she let her careful, first-rate research do the talking, rather than let prejudice against her get in the way.

James Watson and Francis Crick found a challenging problem to solve, and they stuck to it. If solving the problem meant they had to learn about different kinds of chemistry and other things, they learned them. Their work paid off in a breakthrough discovery. As these people found out, science can involve false ideas, confusing facts, and even problems with co-workers. But they didn't let that stop them. And there is a lot of work left to do.

> Watson and Crick's work paid off in a breakthrough discovery.

Scientists "read" DNA sequences, such as this one, to identify particular genes.

Atom
tiniest unit of matter that has the characteristics of an element

Chemical
substance with a definite composition made up of one or more elements

Chromosome
long strand of DNA where genes are found

DNA
substance in cells that contains hereditary information

Dominant trait
trait that masks the influence of a recessive trait when the two appear together

Double helix
spiral shape of DNA resembling a gently twisting ladder

Fertilize
to make something able to bear offspring

Gene
segment of DNA on a chromosome that carries instructions for how a living thing grows and changes

Genetic engineering
changing the genetic makeup of a cell or a living thing by changing, adding, or removing one or more genes

Helix
spiral form

Heredity
passing traits from parents to offspring through genes

Molecule
substance made when two or more atoms bond

Nucleic acid
any of a group of essential complex acids that makes up the genetic material of all living cells

Recessive trait
trait whose characteristics do not appear when combined with a dominant trait

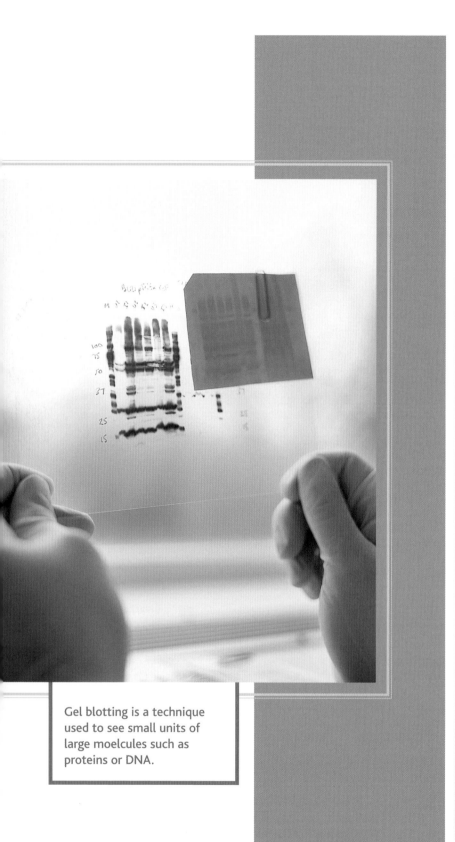

Gel blotting is a technique used to see small units of large moelcules such as proteins or DNA.

Other Cool Stuff on DNA

The Web site for the Marian Koshland Science Museum of the National Academy of Sciences, www.koshland sciencemuseum.org, is a great place for even more information on DNA and how it works. There, you can explore the many roles DNA plays in our lives through interactive activities, including "Catch a Criminal" and "Identify the Disease."

Visit The Gene Scene at http://ology.amnh.org/ genetics/. There, you can create your own DNA model and even print DNA stationery.

To unravel the mystery of DNA's code, visit the DNA learning center at www.dnai. org/a/index.html.

Discover all about genetics at a great site made just for you. See www.genetics.gsk.com/kids/ index_kids.htm.

Having trouble understanding DNA? Try visiting http://www. genecrc.org/site/ko/ko1a.htm where you can get more information and play cool games like "chromosome hunt."

Visit http://www.eurekscience.com/I CanDoThat/dna_structure.htm where "Gene" and "Polly the protien" will teach you more about DNA and its bases.

For simple and easy-to-understand information about the story of DNA, go to http://www.thetech.org/exhibits _events/online/genome/.

What More Can I Do?

Now it's time for a cool experiment. Want to be able to actually see the DNA of an onion? Get an adult to help you, and visit http://ology. amnh.org/genetics/stufftodo/ blender.html for the experiment's instructions.

Would you like to learn more about the amazing Human Genome Project? Visit www. genome.gov/education/ for background information on the project, as well as to learn about National DNA Day!

To get a simple and interesting overview of genetics visit https://www3.nationalgeographic. com/genographic/overview.html.

Wouldn't it be fun to watch animation that explains how DNA replicates? Go to http://www.bioteach.ubc.ca/Teac hingResources/MolecularBiology/ DNAReplication.html and click "DNA replication" to watch.

Also, try heading out to your local science museum or library for more information and fun facts.

RESOURCES

Yellow indicates illustrations.

Atoms
    defined 55
    in DNA 20, 32

Bacteria 21, 21
Brno, Czech Republic
    monastery 12, 14–15

Cambridge, England 8–9,
    24–25, 27–29, 49
Chemicals
    defined 55
    in DNA 41
Chromosomes
    defined 55
    link to heredity 20
Crick, Francis
    biography 23
    birth of 22, 23
    brain research 23, 49
    childhood 23, 26
    death of 53
    discovery of DNA structure
        9, 11, 28, 46, 51, 53
    DNA research 25–29,
        31–33, 35–41
    interest in science 23, 26,
        56
    Nobel Prize 28, 46, 47, 56
    photographs of 8–9, 23,
        26, 32, 37, 47
Criminals, identifying
    role of DNA 11, 50, 57
Cross-breeding 15

Darwin, Charles 15
De Vries, Hugo 17

Diseases
    causes of 19, 31, 51
    cures for 11, 51
    study of DNA 11, 51
    see also Measles
DNA (deoxyribonucleic acid)
    ability to copy itself 32, 41
    defined 11, 55
    discovery of structure 9,
        11, 28, 46, 51, 53
    information carried by 11,
        55
    models 37, 38, 39, 40, 41
    substance name 20
    x-ray photos 38, 39, 39
Dominant traits
    defined 55
    Mendel's experiments 16
Double helix
    defined 55
    DNA shape 39, 40

Fertilize
    defined 55
Franklin, Rosalind
    biography 30
    birth of 27, 30
    death of 30, 46
    DNA research 25, 29–31,
        36, 38–40
    letters written by 56
    photograph of 30
    virus studies 30, 50
    x-ray photo by 39

The Gene Scene (Web site) 57
Genes
    defined 55
    first use of word 22
    made of DNA 20, 21, 28
    Mendel's "factors" 16, 22

Genetic engineering 51, 55
Griffith, Frederick 21, 21

Helix
    defined 55
    DNA shape 33
    see also Double helix
Heredity
    defined 55
Human Genome Project 23, 50,
    57

Johannsen, Wilhelm 22

King's College, London, England
    28, 29, 30, 50

Marian Koshland Science
        Museum, Washington, D.C.
        57
Measles 19, 46
Medicines 11, 19, 51
Mendel, Gregor
    pea plant experiments 11,
        12, 13–17, 20, 53
    photographs of 11, 15
Molecules
    defined 55
    DNA molecule 20, 39, 41

National Academy of Sciences
    57
National DNA Day 57
Nature (journal) 40
Nobel Prizes 23, 28, 33, 46, 46,
    47, 47, 56
Nuclear weapons 22, 33, 46
Nucleic acid
    defined 55
    sugars 20

Onion experiment 57

Pauling, Ava Helen 33
Pauling, Linus
    biography 33
    birth of 20, 33
    childhood 33
    death of 53
    DNA research 31, 36, 38
    models and drawings 31, 31,
        38
    Nobel Prizes 33, 46
    photographs of 33, 49
    textbooks 27
Pea plants 11, 12, 13, 14–15,
        15
    shortness trait 15, 16
    tallness trait 15, 16
Pitchfork, Colin 50

Recessive traits
    defined 55
    Mendel's experiments 16
Ribose 20

Salk Institute 49

Traits and variation 11, 14–15,
        16, 22

Watson, James
    biography 23
    birth of 23, 27
    childhood 23
    discovery of DNA structure
        9, 11, 23, 28, 46, 51, 53
    DNA research 25, 27–29,
        31–33, 35–41, 36
    Nobel Prize 28, 46, 47, 56
    photographs of 8–9, 23, 27,
        32, 37, 47

Wilkins, Maurice
    biography 28
    birth of 22, 28
    childhood 28
    death of 28, 53
    DNA research 25, 28–31,
        35–36, 38–40
    Nobel Prize 28, 46, 47
    photographs of 28, 47
World War II 10, 23, 27, 28

X-rays 28–29, 30, 31, 38, 39,
        47, 50

INDEX

Large parts of this book were previously
published as *Uncovering the Structure of
DNA* (National Geographic Reading
Expeditions), copyright © 2003.

Book design by KINETIK. The body
text of the book is set in Bliss Regular.
The display text is set in Filosofia.

Library of Congress
Cataloging-in-Publication Data

Phelan, Glen.
Double helix: the quest to uncover
the structure of DNA / by Glen Phelan.
p. cm. —(Science quest)
Includes bibliographical references
and index.
Trade ISBN–10: 0-7922-5541-0
Trade ISBN–13: 978-0-7922-5541-3
Libray ISBN–10: 0-7922-5542-9
Libray ISBN–13: 978-0-7922-5542-0
1. DNA—Juvenile literature. 2. DNA—
Research—History—Juvenile literature.
3. Molecular biology—History—Juvenile
literature. I. Title. II. Science quest
(National Geographic Society (U.S.))
QP624.P482 2006
572.8'633—dc22

2005035043

Photo Credits: Cover: © Mehau
Kulyk/Photo Researchers; 4: © Ken
Edward/BioGrafx/Photo Researchers; 6:
© Martin Jones/Corbis; 8-9: © Cold
Spring Harbor Laboratory Archives; 10: ©
Bettmann/Corbis; 11: © Bettmann
/Corbis; 12-13: © James King-
Holmes/Science Photo Library/Photo
Researchers; 14: © Bettmann/Corbis; 15
(left and right): © Bettmann/Corbis; 17:
© Bettmann/Corbis; 18-19: © Steve
Taylor/Getty Images; 20: © Coneyl
Jay/Getty Images; 21 (top): reprinted
with permission Elsevier Science (The
Lancet, 1941, pp. 588-589); 21 (bottom):
© BSIP/Photo Researchers; 22: ©
Bettmann/Corbis; 23: © Bettmann/
Corbis; 24-25: © Michael S. Yamashita
/Corbis; 26: © Hulton Archive/Getty
Images; 27: © Cold Spring Harbor
Laboratory Archives; 28 (top): © The
Dmitri Baltermants Collection/ Corbis;
28 (bottom): © Bettmann/Corbis; 29: ©
London Aerial Photo Library/Corbis; 30
(top): © James Whitmore/ Time & Life
Pictures/ Getty Images; 30 (bottom): ©
Photo Researchers; 31: From the Ava
Helen and Linus Pauling Papers, Special
Collections, Oregon State University; 32:
© A. Barrington Brown/Photo
Researchers; 33: © Science Photo
Library/Photo Researchers; 34-35: © M.

Freeman/Photolink/Getty Images; 36: ©
SuperStock/ Jupiter Images; 37: © A.
Barrington Brown/Science Photo Library
/Photo Researchers; 38: © Michael
Simpson/Getty Images; 39: © Science
Source/Photo Researchers; 40: © Hulton
Collection/Getty Images; 41: © Clive
Freeman/The Royal Institution/Photo
Researchers; 42-43: © Laguna Design/
Photo Researchers; 44-45: © Seth Resnick
/Getty Images; 46: © Bettmann /Corbis;
47: © Bettmann/Corbis; 48: © David
Parker/Photo Reseachers; 49: From the Ava
Helen and Linus Pauling Papers, Special
Collections, Oregon State University; 50: ©
Tek Image/Science Photo Library/Photo
Researchers; 51: © Daisuke Morita/Getty
Images; 52: © Monty Rakusen/Getty
Images; 53: © Bettmann/ Corbis; 54-55: ©
Rob Atkins/Gettty Images; 56: © Steve
Taylor/ Getty Images.